STAYING LOCAL
A pictorial selection for days out
Around the mid South West
By
Terry Hitchcox

Published By
TWHITCH PUBLISHING
57 Alexandra Road
Yeovil, Somerset
BA21 5AL

www.twhitchpublishing.com

© Terry Hitchcox 2015

ISBN 978-0-9559338-9-9

First published in 2016

Printed by Flaydemouse Media Limited
www.flaydemouse.com

Forward

Photography has an obsessional, narcissistic, ecstatic character. It is a solitary activity. The photographic image is irreparable, as irreparable as the state of things at a particular moment. All retouching, all repentance, has, like all posing, an abominably aesthetic character. The solitude of the photograph subject in space and time is correlative with the solitude of the subject and its temperamental silence.

Words from Jean Baudrillard state an opinion that the subject of the photograph is in control of the photographer rather than vice versa. A point he further expands on–

Where does the objective magic of photography come from? The answer is that it is the object that does all the work. Photographers will never admit it, and always argue that all the originality lies in their vision of the world. This is how they take photos that are too good, confusing their subjective vision with the reflex miracle of the photographic act.

The argument here can be extended to question as to the awareness of the object that it exists at all? The photographer at least can see the potential of a subject even though that subject generally has to maintain some reality to be recognisable to the viewer of the image. The reasons for even considering post modern ideas, such as those expounded on by Baudrillard, come from belonging to a camera club where ones efforts can be critically analysed in competition; the variable responses from judges always make me think "why did I take the picture?" The thought process activated by this question usually takes me to ask, "What is reality, is it my idea or theirs?" which moves on then to the philosophical, ontological thinking: - is being a manifestation of something or nothing? After all this mentally mind-boggling meandering, photography still comes down to the action of – We came, we saw, we snapped.

This record of the regular ramifying ramblings undertaken by a pair of proactive, pension possessing photographers has as much to do with coming to terms with having the time for such activity, as it does with the actual art of seeking the pictorial image. The technicalities involved in the hobby of photography have changed dramatically in a single generation; the advent of digital equipment turns almost all who use it into producers of pictures that are *too good.* With this thought in mind what can a be done to make the visual record either stand out as individual images exemplifying the photographers artistic ability or, move away from that idea in which the object itself is demanding to be recognised as a worthy subject?

1

It was during the month of October 2011 that two aging explorers set out to gain an appreciation of the local landscapes and, more significantly, learn to use their cameras to better document what was seen. Having been associated with the Yeovil Camera Club for a few years and observing many presentations, which included a broad spectrum of topics and techniques, the pair fancied emulating what had been seen at the weekly meetings. The mix of professional and amateur photographers certainly gave the impression that although thousands of budding camera-using enthusiasts exist, there was a common theme whereby most seemed to visit a limited range of iconic photogenic sites. Though tempted to follow suit it was decided that any chosen route would tend to towards taking journeys into unknown back roads, looking through the gaps in the hedgerows; turning left or right just following instincts.

Venturing eastwards from Yeovil towards Wincanton there is a stand out characteristic of the landscape visible from the A303, namely Cadbury Hill Fort. This was an area often seen in passing but that day it was considered, worthy of closer attention. Skirting the base of the fort on narrow lanes, then, on climbing an adjacent hill, a view was found which added another perspective that enhanced appreciation of the medieval feature. The flat top of the fort, when seen within its surrounding countryside, became an obvious choice as a defensive position; and when pictured from the neighbouring hill also became the subject of a memorable image. Not only is the pictorial scene inspirational, there is the inconclusively suggested history that we could be seeing the site of Camelot, a legendary centre of power in the dark ages.

In considering the question whether the picture exists because of the realistic demands of the subject or the photographer's perception on finding the best viewpoint is open to interpretation; the evidence in this instance suggests the one who looked back from the car wins.

Shortly after the visit to Cadbury it was time to break for a picnic lunch. Finding another hilltop with a gateway each side of the narrow road became the stopping place of choice. The sun drenched panoramic view across a patchwork of fields contained within low stonewalls became another reason that the day out just got better and better. Especially with what happened next making the argument about a realistically demanding subject coming to life right beside us. On an aluminium gate not ten foot from the car, the rustling of feathers made us turn to see a red-legged partridge sitting atop the bars. The bird insisted that we drop our Scotch egg and Pringles and get snapping, the resulting picture below says it all.

The day was only just beginning and by the time we headed for our respective homes a wide range of subjects had presented themselves for our cameras to record. With no particular place to go we turned whichever way looked suitable for random photography. On a fairly long and straight 'B' road the horses seen below were spotted running at speed along the length of a large field; opportunism had us accelerating to a gated entrance ahead of the advancing equine herd, once again we had a subject for the cameras to do their thing.

The day had started with the intention of finding landscapes that took advantage of having a big blue sky scattered with wispy white cloud, yet we mostly found farm animals queuing up to be given a pictorial life beyond their food producing years.

The day ended when passing through Milborne Wick where the above derelict wheel added rustic charm to the old stone mill house found nestling in a variegated green canopy.

Earlier the question of reality's place in photography was considered and subsequently sidestepped by deferring to 'I came, I saw, I snapped'.

After reference to a few more points of view, while revisiting some of my own pictures, there appeared to be a worthwhile purpose in investigating what is being achieved by my own efforts in respect to representing realism.

There could be a use here for numerous quotes from, and name-dropping of, philosophical thinkers, but it seems a consensus of opinion is that reality has more to do with perception than physical consistency. Photography adds further dimensions to the mix by determining an image is only relevant to the moment of its creation; coupled with the complication in which each viewer of the image has only their own experience to comprehend its significance. Therefore if a photograph is seen without its histogram can it ever be given a time that reasons ambient conditions, or if an unknown object, named regarding its particular situation?

An example of trying to quantify a particular picture, giving a meaning, time and a place, is challenging even to the most erudite of viewers. Below is what can be seen as a possible landscape or perhaps, to those who have flown over a storm, clouds observed from above at 30000ft. In fact this picture was taken using a Canon SX30 set at a maximum 140x zoom looking into the streak of sunset shown in the second picture below; without a positive reference the cloud scene becomes whatever the viewer makes of it.

Another problem of deciding where to focus, or how to set a shot, can crop up in nearly all photographic situations particularly when in failing light as featured in the lower picture above. Use available light? Use flash to highlight the foreground figure? Zoom into a specific detail? Does this mean more decisions, any of the above would produce an image that could be seen as justified, but against what criteria should the choice be made?

At this point it is time to consider not only the cameraman's personality, but also the intellectual and artistic prowess of the viewer. All of which comes into the possible understanding of the image and whether the intent of the photographer can be discerned and appreciated; does it matter if that information remains obscure? Should the operator of the camera give title to their image to aid transferring ideas?

Whoever invented the digital camera has much to answer for, making my brain to work like this. Right time now to go back to basics; who needs to know all these things anyhow?

The scene above was observed on a summer's evening at Ham Hill; a site regularly used by locals for taking pictures of a big-sky sunset.

3

A promising display with more colours shows the advance of the autumn season. The pictures seen here are of Fifehead Wood, next to Fifehead Magdalen in deepest north Dorset. The shades of orange and yellow are left behind when the summer green departs the leaves, letting the natural colours, such as carotene; get us camera-toting people out into the woods. I think Michael, as he was wearing a red top, had a desire to be in the pictures too.

At a camera club meeting last evening the topic of landscape photography was discussed. Part of the subject matter referred to suggestions that can be applied to improve the quality of a picture. The most important of which concentrated on placing the focal point of a picture on the thirds. The two images featuring people in red follow this rule; it's up to you to consider whether this makes those pictures any more pleasurable to look at? This imperative has been talked about so much in photography competitions etc, it becomes automatic to look at the possible shot from this perspective first; the picture below uses the law but it's the colours that do it for me.

Moving on to Shaftsbury a short distance from the wood, gives us the pleasure of being able to visit Gold Hill; oldies like us remember it famously seen in the Hovis advert back in the sixties. The town certainly dominates the high ground as it is built on land over 700 feet above sea level. It was good to see the view was definitely a tourist attraction, a large park gardens takes advantage of a lofty position overlooking part of the Blackmore Vale. The overall outlook to the south was not so easy to capture due to the low December sun behind a skin of misty white cloud,

4

Taking a journey to the south west of Yeovil started well with a clear blue sky and hopefully a good light for taking pictures of wildlife on water. Once again Michael and I were going to test our selves against the prevailing conditions of unpredictable winter weather. On arrival at the approach road to Sutton Bingham reservoir we stopped on a hill overlooking the meandering stretch of water. Here we found the first problem of the day, the sun mistified the view we wished to capture.

At least some gulls found us in the fog but not sure why there was a queue?

One redeeming factor was that the stillness of air meant reflections could be used to enhance our pictures almost to perfection; at least we hoped that wasn't being too optimistic a word?

The visit to Exmoor described here didn't actually involve Michael but since this has proved to be one of the most visited pages on my Wordpress Blog it is included almost in its entirety.

On August 16th 1952 a storm deposited nine inches of rain in two days on Exmoor. A vast amount of the water naturally followed a route to the sea via the East and West Lyn rivers, which came together in a valley that led into Lynmouth; a coastal town on the Bristol Channel.

The map above shows the deep gorges where the rivers run towards Lynmouth, unfortunately the rushing torrent picked up trees and rocks on the journey creating several temporary dams at the sites of many small bridges. As the pressure built the dams gave way releasing an inland tidal wave that wiped out over a hundred homes and killed thirty-four in the town. The reason this event is being talked about here is to acknowledge the depth of feeling that still remains in the older generation's consciousness; I was only seven at the time but memory of the newspaper, black and white TV, and cinema newsreel images stayed with me. Stark reminders of those images were brought up to date 52 years later when on August 16th 2004 seven inches of rain created a similar event at Boscastle in Cornwall; there too a hundred houses were damaged but fortunately nobody died.

Watersmeet is not an accidental naming for a place where two extensive gorges guide water into a single channel forming the East Lyn River. The National Trust, who owns the site, maintains access roads and Watersmeet House, which is used as an information centre and tearoom.

Watersmeet is a place of rugged natural beauty and the thought that this scene of tranquillity can be turned into a maelstrom causing such devastating results as the Lynmouth flood brings on a considered respect for the power of nature. We were there on a relatively quiet day with average, seasonal water levels. The point to note is how the cutting power of the river has carved a channel through solid rock.

The road to Lynmouth runs parallel to the river and requires a regular use of the brakes; fast moving water only has limited friction to check its speed, no wonder at times it becomes unstoppable.

6

To the south of Yeovil is the county borderline with North Dorset and the imposing Babylon hill. The views seen here are taken from an attic bedroom that affords the benefit of being able to witness the full years sunrises. The most civilised timing for this is, from my own preference, in December and January, as seen at about 8am this particular morning. The range of colours to be discerned is quite spectacular, which, when juxtaposed to the first glimpse of the sun create scenes well worth climbing the staircase to see. Once again the question of where to point the lens has to be considered, but this time the answer was to take as many shots and from as many positions to capture the stunning colour show.

7

Out and about again with Michael takes us to the Somerset city of Wells, a place of renown due to the cathedral and the adjoining bishop's palace. There is not much need of a commentary as the quality of the workmanship coupled with buildings sizeable presence can be seen easily from the photographs.

At the side of the cathedral is the bishop's palace that has the unusual attribute of being surrounded by a moat. Luckily the day we went conditions prevailed to get reasonable reflections, which enhanced our photographic efforts.

8

Now it's quiz time and the horse is asking, "What's my line?

You can get an answer from the horse's mouth, or maybe from nearer the horses tail?

Today we are on the Grand Western Canal where the Tiverton Canal Company run the last horse drawn barge in the West Country.

23

My line is a rope.

9

Moving on to another day out for Michael and me begins with a drive to somewhere we know not, but let's go anyway. On our route south we pass Yeovil Junction Station where there was half a chance we might see a visiting steam engine, stopping here for maintenance and to use the turntable. Luckily a sign of activity was visible as we neared attracted to a finger of smoke reaching high into the sky.

The visitor we could see was King Edward 1st, a classic Great Western engine being used to give local students experience of riding and sensing what it was like to travel on a steam train.

To finish the experience for the students, the engine was disconnected from the carriages and moved off to a turntable, which then reversed the steaming workhorse ready for its return journey back to London.

Another lucky moment for photography was a day at Charmouth on the Jurassic Coast of Dorset. Our rear fence neighbour, Chris, organises fossil hunting walks on the beach there. He kindly offered to take us down for the day and let us join his group of rock hammer wielding explorers. The sun was low in the sky and made conditions quite awkward for taking clear pictures out to sea, but fortunately some are reasonable enough to show here. The first shot is of our guide in his beach clambering kit waiting for the customers to book tickets.

The world famous beach has a few areas where cliff face landslides happen regularly, Charmouth is noted as good for fossil hunting, but be careful when under the cliffs. The best time to search is just as the high tide turns with the water leaving behind freshly washed pebbles making it easier to identify those concealing fossils within.

The hunting was not the only activity at the waters edge as the selection of pictures shows:

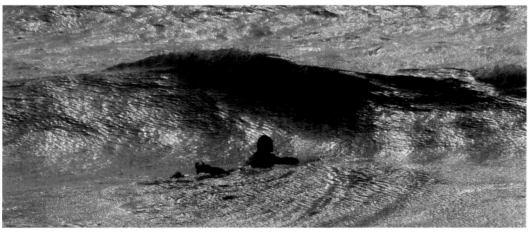

11

Michael and me are out again for our seemingly monthly photofest day, heading a bit further west. Starting with a brief stop beside the River Axe, just before it mingles with the waters of the English Channel. Once again the weather was fair for our trip but the mist was still taking some time to be burnt off by a not quite hot enough sun. As can be seen in the following pictures this is a popular place for a multitude of Gull families to rear their young.

Looking south the river moves on to enter the sea beside the coastal town of Seaton, unfortunately the parking there is not easy on busy sunny days so we moved on to the oddly named town of Beer. It sits on the coast a few miles west of Seaton; a notable variety of stone has been used when building up the mainly attractive centre, seen here after parking close to the beach.

Checking out the facilities here we found the range of food to be a bit narrow as not many places were open due to the uncertainty of the March weather, time to move on to Sidmouth, a short drive away. The mist here was very evident but we still managed to get a few worthwhile shots.

Once again enough pictures had been acquired to tell this story of the day, we also observed a selection of the fellow sun lovers in various styles of clothes and poses.

To finish it is time for one of my favourites of the day, taken on the bank of the Axe where a tiny brook was meeting up with the river in a very photogenic way.

Contaminated' Sutton Bingham reservoir drained

A water reservoir in Somerset has been partially drained after traces of pesticides were found in it. Owners Wessex Water said tests carried at Sutton Bingham towards the end of January revealed low levels of pesticide residue from slug pellets. Spokesman Luke de Vial said as a precaution the reservoir and associated treatment works was taken out of service.

Considering the above article in the local paper inspired Michael and me to revisit the nearby reservoir to see if the drop in the water level had attracted birds and animals that might like waddling in mud. When we saw that the height of the lake was at about half full, the changes in wild life activity were noted to be only very slight. As can be seen in the pictures below some of the normal lake bed had surfaced as a small island which, in turn, was covered by a conglomeration of cormorants; with the usual sight of grebes drifting and diving in the wind swept waters.

On the bank at the east end of the reservoir lived dobbinesses 1 and 2 who, as animals I usually wish to photograph, stayed unhelpfully in grazing mode; though one did come to the fence for a quick pat on the head. On the way home we stopped on a hill near the village of Closworth where the sun played hide and seek, but did come out a couple of times allowing us to take the pictures of the shadows which added a new dimension to enhance normal scenic shots.

13

It was to be a testing time in attempting to take reasonable photographs when the weather could be called inclement, or as we say in the profession it was raining. Not wishing to travel any great distance in these conditions Michael and Me decided to prepare for an exhibition due later in the summer that had a theme of images of the Somerset village of Montacute, situated only a couple of miles west of Yeovil.

Our visit to Montacute centred on St Catherine's, a building that typified the size, style and architecture of a provincial English church. The capacity for bums on pews is rarely different for the type of churches seen, mainly due to the fact that nearly every village has one; even though they may be only a mile or two apart. Michael is a vicar and has five churches in his keeping, all of which are within a five-mile radius.

As can be seen in the above pictures, the craftsmanship and TLC used in the creation and ongoing maintenance is more than evident. The problem is the drop in attendance coupled with the ever-increasing cost of repairs has been the cause for many of these buildings to be sold and converted into village halls, or private housing. One thing that did go our way, unfortunately not a change in the weather, was that Michael arranged for us to gain access to the tower and the roof; yes you could say he had friends in high places. From there we could appreciate the view of the village, farmhouses and the imposing Montacute House.

To our surprise when up the tower we saw three alpaca looking very bedraggled in the field behind the church,, the brown one manage to smile though.

41

14

The morning weather was diabolical, an inch of rain in a very short time, overcast and really not a day to be out taking pictures; but I was with Michael. Somehow when we team up to gather images apt moments present themselves and there are enough photographs to produce a post. My neighbour, Carl, helps out at the nearby Wincanton Racecourse with the advantage that friends can gain access to take pictures; Michael and I were able to take up the opportunity.

The first race was not till 6pm so we left early to look for photo ops' on the way. A theme presented itself very quickly as we found worthy subjects of an equine nature after only a short drive.

It was a shame about the white sky but the attractiveness of the animals gave purpose to the effort; now on to the reason for the journey.

The reason for our visit to Wincanton was to try and capture the essence of the day in camera, but for others there existed a far more important purpose – money!

Course side betting, no names, no records, just the hopeful expectation that today was the day luck would be with the punter; unfortunately no exotic holidays for me this year, my horses are still running. Before each race the competing horses were shown so comparisons could be made by those there to gamble and secondly to award prizes for the best presented.

The races were started in various places around the course with the finishing post in front of the main stand, the position of the start being determined by the lengths of race to be run. The area used for the course can be seen here as extensive enough to have a golf course contained within the track.

The view from the seated stand (?) took in most of course with the quality of the horses determining whether they used hurdles or jumps as obstacles to be negotiated; both can be seen in use below.

Racing over it was then time to head for home, on the journey we were greeted by the spectacular skies and scenery seen below; I told you things happened when out with Michael.

Would we go again? You bet we would.

15

A quiet Saturday afternoon in the country watching cricket, the sound of leather against willow echoing around the nearby buildings to our lofty position up another church tower; out with Michael again this time at Chilton Cantello school. Yes a nice peaceful interlude – NOT!

Michael's connection with the church gave us access to the tower, which, fortunately overlooked part of the local navel air station runway; and today was time for the Yeovilton Air show. Soon after we had climbed the hundred odd steps to the top, a deep throated jet engine could be heard slowly approaching from the west of the tower. Coming our way was a Russian ANTONOV 240, one of the biggest transport planes in the world that can carry over 130 tons of payload. Quite an impressive show as can be seen here.

It was a pity that due to Michael's having to create a union that no one could put asunder we missed a large part of the show, but still managed to see things worth climbing the tower for. Next up to give a lengthy display were two early jets from the fifties: a Sea Venom, with the twin boom; and a Gloster Meteor, a sequel and similar design to the Gloster Whittle, the first ever jet plane created at the end of WW2.

The first picture below shows a flight of six trainers belonging to Saudi Arabia; their job was to entertain us with a aerobatic display almost equal to the famous Red Arrows, who had performed before we arrived.

It was a pity the weather had not been too kind, the light not really bright enough to be able to attain sharp pictures; but this is why we work in all conditions, to try and get the best from our cameras.

The last image below is an aerial view our road home to Yeovil, which is just over the hill at the top right of the picture.

16

Heading to North Somerset with friends Carl and Di, there was an opportunity to capture scenes of 'chocolate box cover' notoriety. The village of Selworthy sits on a hill overlooking the valley that enters the sea at Porlock, and a dramatic change in the landscape with the steep rise up to Exmoor, producing a photogenic background to our pictures.

A church sits atop the village with commanding views of the surrounding countryside, but is in itself well worthy to be in Selworthy.

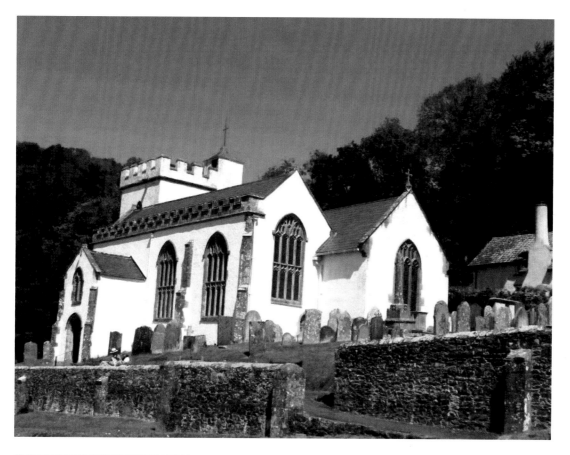

Most of Selworthy is nestled among trees as it surrounds well-manicured lawns acting as an extended village green.

Carl and Di are seen here enjoying morning coffee at the Periwinkle Cottage tea room, not only observed by the camera, but also a resident blackbird very used to being with us visitors. E sees I and I sees E.

The satisfying repast over with it was time to move on, Porlock Weir harbour and the famous Porlock hill were beckoning.

Blue sky = blue sea, what a way to get an indifferent, inclement May out the way. Only problem is it's forecast for one day only, cold and wet predicted for the rest of the week.

In the words of James Cagney, in the film White Heat – "Made it Ma, top of the hill" almost 2000 feet above sea level; fortunately this was not an exploding gasometer like which done Cagney in. Also we were some way from any cliffs, so no suspense here, but at least your reading this. Thanks to my camera there are things to see when zooming in, first here is a farmhouse seen as a speck at the bottom of the hill, secondly there was a freighter some way off on the coast of Wales.

Looking inland the scenery changed to a more rugged appearance with heathers and gorse a major part of the vegetation. The sweep of deep valleys cut into the high plateau highlighting the contrast with Selworthy only a few miles down the road.

After a lunch of locally made pasties and apple cake we descended into the Doone valley, its well-watered lush flora adding another aspect to the picture show.

No matter where we go, sheep and ponies everywhere.

Finishing with the awwww factor.

17

I spy with my little eye something beginning with 'R'. For the second time in a week one's photographic skill is being put to the test by the adverse weather; I think the pictures are reasonable – just!

Today Michael and me were heading south to the Dorset coast and the sights of Corfe Castle and the resort of Swanage, an area I had not seen close up since camping there with the Boys Brigade back in the mid 1950s. On the way near the town of Blandford we were attracted to the landscape so stopped to record the view.

Even the wet road created an image worth capturing, and then it was onward to Corfe, an historic site surrounded by cottages and streets that appeared to be fitting the period of the ruins.

From Corfe it was only a few miles down to the coastal town of Swanage, a place noted for its curved bay and a backdrop of normally photogenic cliffs; shame about the mist.

The clothing of the natives and most probably the happy holidaymakers displayed what one has to do to survive a rather prolonged wet summer.

After lunch by the seashore we ventured to the high ground overlooking Corfe to try for some atmospheric pictures, but the mist won. A distant plume of smoke told us that the steam train between our two destinations was running today so we descended the hill to get closer. On approaching the station, near the Castle, an unexpected bonus presented itself in the guise of a lesser-spotted woodpecker taking advantage of a birdfeeder filled daily by the car park attendant.

18

As a follow up to the part display seen previously pictures from an earlier air show at Yeovilton have been included here as compensation for what was missed. We saw a wide range of aircraft giving a good account of what they do best, but before the planes took to the air the sky was littered with the canopied bodies of parachutists floating gently to earth.

After a mixture of other displays we end up seeing a Harrier Jump Jet hovering just in front of the fairground being celebrated as a squadron of them had been stationed at Yeovilton; but now they were being thrown away by our penny pinching and mindless new coalition government. (That's not just my view on the matter).

What followed has to be an example of trusting in your fellow human beings, the strap makers, the strap fixers, the pilots and a belief you are going to make it through the day.

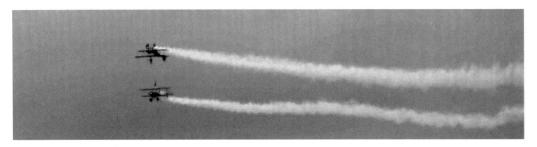

After watching such a brilliant aerobatic display from the Breitling display team the next page will maybe slow things down a bit, or maybe not, readers will just have to check it out.

A short time after the wing walkers stunning show things did get faster, certainly noisier, and somewhat smokier with the arrival of the Red Arrows. The cloud cover was increasing as the afternoon progressed and the display contained more horizontal action than previously witnessed in earlier years.

Job done it was time to go.

Finishing with one of the stars of the show. Pictures were taken from the village of Limington, a mile or so south of the runway, which explains the slight pixilation on some of the zoomed images.

Luckily we had seen a classic collection of aircraft which, when coupled with a blue-sky day, seemed made for creating a worthwhile set of pictures.

19

"If you build it he will come."

This may be a cornflowery start but when you see the pictures they inspire thoughts like these. I may not be Kevin Cosner's dad, well not the father of Ray Kinsella Costner's role in the film 'Field of dreams', but I did get there; and the people came as well.

The dream here though is not about a baseball field, but a flower meadow. The idea of the owners of Barcroft Hall in South Petherton Somerset is used to take donations for charity. Containing almost 60 different wild flowers from around the world almost all are in bloom during July and August, the time when the field is open to the public. As the following pictures show the concept is not about the individual flowers but the effect of combining that many colours, aromas and delicate shapes in one space.

"So much nectar, so little time."

Wyndham Winterland

Once upon a time, not so long ago, in a land not so far away, the weather suggested it was wintertime. The same hill but certainly something different about it. The journey starts outside my house the night before.

May be we will see it again one day?

Making the best of a break in the wet weather Michael and me took to the high ground for some landscape and big sky photography. An opportunity predictably in vision at the local beauty spot of Ham Hill, all looks fine until you look closer at the watery features seen in the distance.

At first glance the small lakes look to be naturally placed within this landscape but anyone who has seen the recent news will know this is certainly not a regular sight seen at this angle. From Ham Hill we moved over to Yeovilton village for a closer look, luckily the roads were clear so access was not a problem. The result of an accumulation of rainwater over the summer and, more pertinently, the heavy storms over the last few weeks was there before our eyes.

The light was playing tricks with us, the pictures above were to our left facing north, and then to our right and into the sun the reflections and the shadows make for a completely different perspective on the scene.

The next two pictures are there to challenge you readers to play spot the difference, the first is a few months old and shows the River Yeo in normal flow; see if you can spot the changes made by adding a bit extra water.

Yes that is the same weir in both pictures.

Next we see the river heading off to the Somerset Levels proper and the scene that greeted us from Langport, which overlooked the main area of flooding.

The last picture is of Muchelney Church, both the press and TV made these type of images world famous; the fact it happened two years running put a great deal of pressure on those whose job it is to protect the local population here.

22

Duck a la orange, blue, white, all sorts really.

Once again a grey day but these colourful Mandarin boys certainly brighten up the lake as they work hard to impress their not so vivid girl friends.

When admiring the Mandarin ducks this week, pictures of an unknown fowl were also taken, when investigated it was identified as a **Blue Winged Goose.** A bird that is incorrectly named as it belongs to the Shell duck family. It apparently comes from Ethiopia and is recognised as a vulnerable species due to diminishing habitat availability. It needs water so we know why this one is here.

23

On the road again finding a picturesque idyll just south of Bath, which has the added interest of the Bristol Avon River and the Kennett and Avon Canal, both going through the town.

No matter where you go in the centre of the town the Catholic Church seems to be in view.

The question of how the building below shown next stays standing does show good reason as to why there is no parking here.

Going north towards Bath, not far from town, is a Mill on the Blog at Avoncliff that has an aqueduct taking the Kennett and Avon Canal over the River Avon.

The jogger in the picture has got it wrong if he is heading for an early Bath, the city is off in the other direction.

24

On our next foray into the surrounding countryside took us south east, taking the road towards Blandford there is a chance to see a cultivated herd of deer; be warned the road is very busy with fast traffic. We did find it hazardous shooting this set of deer pictures from the roadside just past Stock Gaylard House in Dorset.

By accident rather than design, a second viewing of deer was seen on our way home that day. Passing farmland on the road between Bradford Abbas and Yeovil, these deer have been seen a few times before but here they waited for us to take a picture.

The same day we visited Hinton St Mary to enjoy a snack lunch while taking in an attractive landscape in North Dorset. The local church of St Peters is over 500 years old and stands next to a manor house that used to be a nunnery. The avenue of trees is open to the public and even supplied a musical interlude with a resident thrush singing in a treetop above our chosen picnic spot. This proved to be another lucky day for finding places away from the crowds but well worth the effort.

This last picture is a particular favourite that uses a low in the sky sun with great effect.

25

Sturminster Newton

Michael and I revisited the River Stour and were surprised to see how much the water level had dropped. Not long ago when passing by the area the footbridges seen here were impassable due to being enveloped by the recent flooding; the high water mark on the mill says it all.

105

26

Cutt Mill.

Moving on from the Sturminster only a few miles down river is Cutt Mill, a now vandalised and derelict   building destroyed by fire in 2003. Also on the Stour, a sixty-mile long river that starts its journey at Stourhead House, a place visited last November; see blog Autumn Colours in the archive. The surrounding fields were still heavily saturated from the recent floods so most of these pictures were taken from the easily accessible hard ground; at least the sun was out, most likely we will return when conditions improve.

The high water mark on the mill wall again shows the depth of flooding here, no wonder there is a boat beside the farmhouse.

27

As stated at the beginning of this pictorial wandering our usual modus operandi involved following instincts and looking through gaps in the hedgerows to find possible subjects. The last outing featured here is a good example of how Michael and I are lucky when it comes to being inspired by the totally unexpected. Venturing across the nearby Dorset border we head towards Sherborne via the B road passing Bradford Abbas. We have sometimes seen roaming wild deer in the open farmland and slowed to a crawl just in case of a sighting. On the sunny side of the narrow road we came across a newly mown field littered with black plastic covered hay bales; our fingers inched toward the cameras.

We had given ourselves a challenge here as the hazy sky coupled with a horizon enshrouded in mist meant sharp images would not be easy to obtain. Turning partially towards the west and including less of the sky did improve the visible details

It took a short walk down into the field and getting the sun behind us to find a clearer image that also benefitted from a more defined colour contrast.

Moving on we headed upwards into the high ground to the south with the intention of finding a friendlier sky by seeing this valley from a better angle. On the way we still found a few sights worthy of our time.

Still using back roads gave us an unexpected present in the shape of a gathering of pheasants meandering leisurely up a shallow hill, not concerned at all with us following at a discreet distance.

That sighting had gone seriously towards making our day, but once we had climbed to the top of Batcombe hill we nearly missed the chance to see a grazing herd of alpaca behind a heavily fenced farm entrance.

Even though the sighting of these animals is becoming more common it is seemingly imperative that the almost comical faces are demanding us to stop and take the picture.

The question raised in the forward to this pictorial expedition, that highlights some of the attractions to be seen when exploring the area around my hometown of Yeovil, may be answered by considering the pictures themselves. It is regularly stated that beauty is to be found fundamentally in the eye of the beholder, whether that observer is the cameraman or the viewer of the image is a query that needs further consideration. The obvious conclusion would be to say that both have opinions of merit, but is there a need for a decision actually to be made?

Also available in the Terry Hitchcox series of books

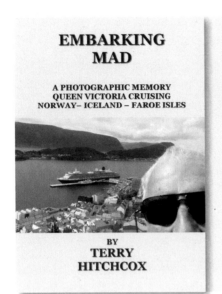

Embarking Mad

88 pages
ISBN Paperback: 978955933844
ISBN E-Book: 780955933851

Witnessing White Star service on six separate sailings my wife Jane and I are appreciative of being shown every respect by Cunard's staff. In addition those we came in touch with either daily or only once, displayed a friendliness that cruising this way promotes a classless plural microcosm so missing in a modern society where right wing governments are only seeking to endorse a life of selfish greed. This may seem hypocritical when describing a holiday in extreme luxury, but most passengers know this a transitory illusional world where we are Jack and Rose, but the bow of the ship is out of bounds. Nothing wrong with wanting to be king of the world, is there?

USA Our Way

142 pages
ISBN Paperback: 9780955933875
ISBN E-Book: 9780955933806

To some people the holiday story presented here will be seen as an extravagant waste of money, or some might think spending an unexpected windfall this way would be unwise; it could even be considered that to have two trips of a lifetime is positively greedy.

Whichever way, you the reader can decide for yourself; we're just glad we had the combined chances to do it.

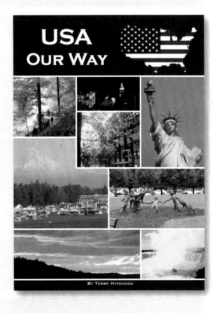

Are You All Right For Saturday?

56 pages
ISBN Paperback: 9780955933820
ISBN E-Book: 9780955933837

This book focuses on the life, and fifty year amateur career of Ron Hitchcox in team building, management and the local league administration.

Written records and interviews with various colleagues helped to show his experiences can be used as an example of the effort and commitment, mostly given away freely, by an army of behind the scenes organisers in youth and junior football.

www.twhitchpublishing.com